SERIES 208

In this book we will travel
from the coastline to the ocean depths,
visiting mudflats, tropical coral reefs and icy
Antarctic waters to discover the amazing
marine creatures that make oceans
their home.

LADYBIRD BOOKS
UK | USA | Canada | Ireland | Australia
India | New Zealand | South Africa
Ladybird Books is part of the Penguin Random House group of companies
whose addresses can be found at global.penguinrandomhouse.com
www.penguin.co.uk   www.puffin.co.uk   www.ladybird.co.uk.

Penguin
Random House
UK

First published 2020
001
Copyright © Ladybird Books Ltd, 2020
Printed in China
A CIP catalogue record for this book is available from the British Library
ISBN: 978-0-241-41707-2
All correspondence to:
Ladybird Books
Penguin Random House Children's
One Embassy Gardens, New Union Square
5 Nine Elms Lane, London SW8 5DA

MIX
Paper from
responsible sources
FSC® C018179
www.fsc.org

Sea Creatures

A Ladybird Book

Written by Hannah Pang
with marine consultant, Dr Shannon Leone Fowler

Illustrated by Amber Davenport

Tidal rock pool

When waves and rain lash against the coastline, small pools of water collect in hollows in the rock. Known as "rock pools", these tiny aquariums are home to lots of different creatures of the sea.

The animals in rock pools cope with constant changes to their surroundings, or "environment". The movement of the tide means that nothing stays the same for long. There are food shortages and the temperature, oxygen level and salt content in the water can also change dramatically.

Rock-pool creatures have adapted well to living in this strange space between the land and the open ocean. For example, blue mussels use their shells for protection. They open underwater to feed, and then close tightly when the tide goes out so they don't dry out.

Competition for space in a rock pool is fierce. Slow-moving sea anemones often compete with each other for space and the beadlet anemone will even battle enemies for the right spot using specialized stinging cells.

The common cuttlefish is a master of disguise. It has amazing colour-changing abilities that help it to blend into its surroundings. Because it is camouflaged, it can attack unsuspecting prey, such as brown shrimp.

Crab and conch

Crabs live in the sea, on land and anywhere in-between. They are a type of creature known as a "crustacean". There are over 6,700 crab species in the world, ranging from the tiny pea crab to the giant Japanese spider crab.

Crabs are known as "decapods" because they have ten legs. The front pair develop into strong, gripping claws, which crabs use for defence and to grasp at food or prey. The remaining eight legs are used for walking. Most species of crab have legs that bend out to the side, which means they move in a sideways direction.

Despite its name, the Caribbean hermit crab is not a "true" crab. It does not have a hard outer shell, known as an "exoskeleton". Instead, its body is soft and curved, which makes it a much easier target for predators. To protect itself, this land species must find its own home, so hermit crabs are often found inside old sea snail shells.

This shell would have once belonged to a large sea snail called a "conch". Conchs live in tropical waters, including the Caribbean and Mediterranean. Many predators, such as turtles, sharks and humans, feed on the bodies of the conchs, leaving their shells empty. Hollow shells then wash up on the shore and make perfect homes for larger Caribbean hermit crabs.

Barnacle, whelk and limpet

Clinging to almost any hard surface in the seawater are hundreds of barnacles, limpets and whelks. Barnacles are particularly sticky little crustaceans as they produce one of the most powerful natural glues in the world.

Gathering in clusters, young barnacles attach themselves head first to a hard surface and then build a "calcium palace" around their bodies. These hard, white cones are usually made up of six plates, with extra plates creating a door-like opening. The barnacle will open and close this "door" to feed on tiny floating organisms called "plankton".

The main predators of barnacles are whelks. These meat-eating sea snails use force to open barnacles and inject them with a special chemical that paralyses them. The whelk is then able to open the cone with ease and feast on the barnacle inside.

Limpets are easily identified by their hard, cone-shaped shell and single muscular foot that they use to cling on to the rock. Although the limpet is able to move a little, it always returns to the same spot, using a slime, or "mucus", trail to find its way home. They are also victims of the whelk, although whelks feed slightly differently on limpets than they do barnacles – they drill holes in the limpet's shell before sucking out the contents.

The mudflats

A mudflat is a stretch of land that is regularly flooded by sea or river tides. The frequent movement of the water causes sand, silt and soil to be whipped up and deposited, creating "mud islands". Found in sheltered areas, such as bays, lagoons and estuaries (places where the rivers join the sea), mudflats are a key habitat for migratory seabirds, as well as certain species of crab, mollusc and fish.

Hooded cranes and black-faced spoonbills spend their winter on the mudflats in Suncheon Bay, South Korea. This salty, swampy habitat is an ideal home for snails, fish, worms and aquatic plants, which means it is also an ideal hunting ground for hungry migrating birds. Local villagers travel across the mudflats on carts and wooden boards to harvest sand crabs, cockles, clams and mudskippers for their own dinner.

As well as providing a feast for local wildlife, mudflats also purify water as it heads back into the ocean. As chemicals from factories and homes find their way into waterways, the mud particles of the mudflats act as a natural sieve. They separate and collect the pollution from the water as it drifts along. Mudflats are also excellent flood barriers, as large amounts of water can be absorbed and drained away in the sand and soil.

Sea star

Sea stars are also known as "starfish", despite not actually being fish at all. They do not have scales or fins or even a backbone. This lack of spine means that they belong to the world's largest animal family instead – the invertebrates.

There are approximately 2,000 different species of sea star, found in a variety of habitats all over the world, including rock pools, seashores, coral reefs and the deep ocean. Most sea stars are covered in protective spines and have a number of arms connected to a small, circular body in the centre. Although most sea stars have five arms, some have many more, including the sunflower sea star, which can grow up to 24 arms.

Sea stars are able to regenerate and grow a new arm if they lose one – a useful trick if they are ever injured or need to escape a predator. Sometimes, the lost arm even grows into a whole new sea star!

Sea stars move slowly across the seabed, using hundreds of tiny tube-like feet beneath their bodies. They have eyespots on the end of their arms to sense changes in light, which help them to find food. Although eyespots can't detect much detail, some studies have shown that there are species, such as the blue sea star, that are able to see very rough images.

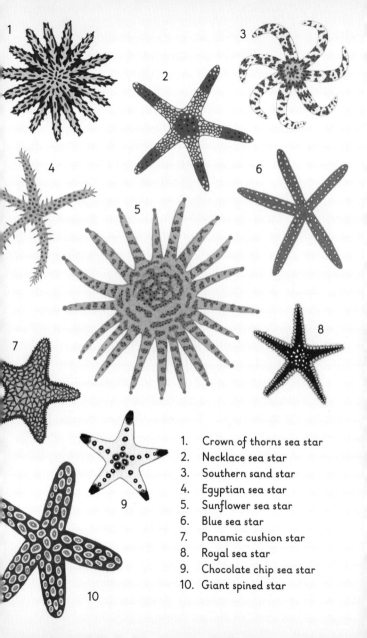

1. Crown of thorns sea star
2. Necklace sea star
3. Southern sand star
4. Egyptian sea star
5. Sunflower sea star
6. Blue sea star
7. Panamic cushion star
8. Royal sea star
9. Chocolate chip sea star
10. Giant spined star

Manatee

Found in the warm, shallow coastal waters of
the Caribbean, Florida and South America, manatees
are unusual-looking sea creatures that are also related
to the elephant and the aardvark. They have been given
the nickname "sea cow" because one adult manatee can
eat more than 50 kilograms (110 lb) of seagrass in a day!

Measuring up to 4.5 metres (15 ft) long and weighing up to
1,400 kilograms (3,100 lb), the West Indian manatee is the
largest living species of sea cow and a threatened species.
As they swim slowly towards the surface of the water, West
Indian manatees are often injured by boat propellers,
caught in fishing nets or hunted.

Despite its size, the manatee has very little fat to keep it
warm – its large body is mostly made up of its intestines!
As such, manatees cannot survive in water that is too cold,
as they cannot produce enough body heat to make up for
heat lost in the cold water. If the water feels a little chilly,
the manatees will migrate somewhere warmer.

A female manatee will usually have just one baby, known
as a "calf", every two to five years. The calf is born
underwater and it is able to swim within minutes of birth.
A calf will stay with its mother, feeding on her milk and
learning about feeding areas and migration routes,
for up to two years.

The Great Barrier Reef

In spite of their plantlike appearance, corals are actually soft-bodied sea creatures. The mound we call "coral" is in fact made up of lots of soft-bodied, tube-shaped creatures known as "polyps".

Hard coral polyps produce a chemical called "calcium carbonate", which hardens to create a protective skeleton and forms the overall structure of a coral reef. The average reef grows less than 2.5 centimetres (1 in.) each year, but over time they can become extremely large.

The Great Barrier Reef is off the east coast of Queensland, Australia, and is the world's largest reef at around 1,400 miles (2,300 km) long. It is home to over 1,500 species of fish, as well as an enormous variety of other sea creatures from giant clams to green sea turtles to yellow-bellied sea snakes.

Special relationships can form between creatures that live in the same environment. Both clownfish and sea anemones live in coral reefs such as the Great Barrier Reef. Clownfish have evolved to grow a very thick layer of mucus around their bodies, so they are able to swim between an anemone's tentacles without getting stung. In return for a secure home, clownfish clean the anemone and chase off any potential predators, such as the butterfly fish.

Kelp forest and sea otter

The most well-known kelp forest runs along the Pacific coast of North America, from Alaska and Canada, to the waters of Baja California, Mexico. These dense patches of kelp grow along rocky shorelines and can be found in cold waters around the world.

Kelp is a large brown alga, or seaweed, that attaches itself to the seabed. It stretches up to the surface, reaching heights of more than 30 metres (100 ft), before spreading out into a floating canopy that shades the seabed below.

Kelp forests are some of the most productive environments on earth. These underwater forests are home to a huge range of animal life, including fish, sea stars, seabirds and marine mammals, like sea otters.

The sea otter can be key to the kelp forest's survival. Large populations of purple sea urchins can spell trouble for the forest, for these urchins feed on the kelp, mowing everything down in their path. They can eat their way through a kelp forest very quickly and prevent regrowth by destroying the area completely. However, sea otters keep the urchin population under control as they eat the urchins as spiky snacks, helping the kelp forest to thrive.

Seahorse

Seahorses live mainly in shallow, tropical and mild or temperate waters, preferring sheltered areas such as seagrass beds, coral reefs and mangroves. Seahorse species can differ dramatically in colour and size, ranging from less than 2 centimetres (0.8 in.) up to 35 centimetres (14 in.) in length. They are also one of the few species where the male gives birth instead of the female.

When ready to mate, male and female seahorses "dance" together for days, often linking their tails. At the end of the dance, the female releases her eggs into a pouch on the male's front. He then carries the babies for nine to 45 days before giving birth to roughly 1,000 live young at a time.

While her partner is pregnant, the female produces even more eggs and so, shortly after the male gives birth, they mate again. By sharing the role in this way, seahorses can produce a high number of young in a short amount of time.

After birth, baby seahorses are left to fend for themselves. At risk of being eaten by predators or being swept away from their feeding grounds by the current, it is estimated that fewer than five infant seahorses out of each 1,000 survive to reach adulthood, which explains the large number of babies per pregnancy.

1. Bullneck seahorse
2. Zebra seahorse
3. Common seahorse
4. Blue seahorse
5. Dwarf seahorse
6. Short-snouted seahorse

Coconut octopus

The coconut octopus is commonly found throughout the tropical Pacific and Indian Oceans, from Australia to South Africa, southern Japan, New Guinea and Indonesia. Like many octopuses, it spends its time on the seabed, but it has an unusual trick to stay out of the way of predators.

Most octopuses use either the colour-changing trick of camouflage to hide from predators or they squirt ink so they can escape. But the coconut octopus carries around two halves of a coconut shell instead, so that it can quickly fold itself inside when it senses danger. This behaviour was only discovered by scientists in 2009. Before witnessing this amazing adaptation, it was thought that the veined octopus (as it was more commonly known) would just hide in nearby shells, not carry them around in preparation.

By collecting shells for future use, the coconut octopus is one of the few animals that uses tools in an intelligent way. This crafty octopus can even use the two halves of the coconut to roll along the ocean floor and speed up its travel!

Octopuses are intelligent creatures and are considered to have nine brains. There is one central brain in the head, and a smaller brain in each of its eight arms. This allows each arm to move independently of the others while still working together as one.

Fish schools and sailfish

Fish in the open ocean often travel together in large groups, numbering in the hundreds or even thousands! Shoaling fish stick together for social reasons. They swim about on their own but always within easy reach of a group, whereas schooling fish swim together in the same direction and at the same speed.

Sardines are tiny schooling fish that migrate in their millions. In fact, the sardine run is one of the largest migrations on earth and it is even visible from the air. At its largest, the school might be 4.3 miles (7 km) long, 1 mile (1.6 km) wide and 30 metres (100 ft) deep.

A school of fish moves as one, changing direction as a whole group in order to confuse predators and to avoid the risk of being singled out as prey. When threatened, sardines group together to form massive ball shapes, known as "bait balls", which can be up to 20 metres (66 ft) wide.

When hunting sardines, the Atlantic sailfish will raise the sail on its back. It swings its long, sharp bill from side to side within the bait ball, picking off and eating the wounded sardines one by one. Sailfish hunt in groups and continually change colour, possibly as a way to communicate with other sailfish and to confuse the prey.

Box jellyfish

The deadly box jellyfish, also known as the "sea wasp", is considered to be the most venomous animal in the world, as it is able to produce a very powerful poison, or "toxin". These transparent, almost-invisible creatures are often found in the tropical oceans north of Australia and throughout the Indo-Pacific region.

They are one of the few jellyfish that can swim, "steer" and actively hunt. Box jellyfish use their long and narrow box-shaped bodies, or "bells", to catch and push out water. This helps them to move up to 2 metres (7 ft) per second.

The tentacles of a fully grown box jellyfish can measure up to 3 metres (10 ft) in length. They have about fifteen tentacles on each box "corner", and each tentacle has about 5,000 stinging cells.

Each of these small cells contains a venom-filled dart that fires whenever the tentacle comes into contact with the chemicals on the surface of its prey. The venom attacks the heart, nervous system and skin cells of its victim. The more the prey tries to shake off the darts, the more the tentacles stick to its skin, releasing even more stingers.

Despite its deadly reputation, the box jellyfish still has predators, such as the green sea turtle, which is immune to the jellyfish venom and able to attack.

Dolphin

Dolphins use a series of clicks and squeaks to observe or "see" the environment around them. This process is called "echolocation". The clicking sounds that dolphins make bounce off nearby objects in echoes and return at different times, angles, pitches and volumes. This provides all the information a dolphin needs, such as the object's distance and size, and whether it is moving or not. Echolocation helps dolphins to find food, navigate their surroundings and become alert to danger – even in the dark.

Dolphins communicate with each other using their own language – also a series of whistles and clicks. Groups, or "pods", of dolphins travel together, and dusky dolphins, found in the southern hemisphere, are the most acrobatic travellers, performing extremely high jumps, twists and flips.

Dusky dolphins are often seen leaping out of the water, or "breaching". Scientists believe they may do this to get a better view of things in the distance – if seagulls are making a fuss then there is likely to be food, or fish, involved! But it may also be a way of communicating and bonding with other dolphins, or saving energy (as air is easier to travel through than water). Some believe that dolphins jump to get rid of any marine worms on their skin. Or it may be that they are simply having fun! The truth is that no one really knows . . .

Manta ray

The giant manta ray is the largest species of ray – a type of flat fish closely related to sharks. However, unlike most fish, rays and sharks have very light skeletons, which are made from cartilage rather than bone. Cartilage is a substance that flexes without breaking. It is the same material that is found in human ears and noses.

Found in tropical and subtropical waters in all of the world's major oceans – as well as many mild, or "temperate", seas – giant manta rays have a particular style of swimming. They propel themselves forward and glide through the water using their large, wing-like fins, called "pectoral fins". This movement makes them appear to fly through water.

The manta's flat body and head also help it to move quickly, as they are aerodynamic in shape. It is also coated in slimy mucus, which not only protects the skin from infection, but reduces any drag through the water. As such, with little resistance, the giant manta is easily able to reach speeds of over 15 miles (24 km) per hour in bursts.

Giant mantas often visit oceanic "cleaning stations". On approach, the manta will open its mouth or position its body in such a way to show that it needs cleaning. Fish, such as cleaner wrasse, will then eat any parasites from the manta's skin – and even those inside its mouth!

Shark pup

The length of a female shark's pregnancy is very changeable. As sharks are cold-blooded creatures, the time it takes for babies, or pups, to develop depends on the water temperature rather than time. Most pups develop somewhere between five and 24 months, depending on the size of the species.

Shark pups can be born in three ways:

1. The pups develop inside the mother, similar to a human baby. When ready, the mother then gives birth to live young.

2. Some sharks lay eggs. These often have a tough, leathery casing, come in a variety of shapes and sizes and are known as a "mermaid's purse". A female shark will try to make sure that its egg is securely fixed in a safe place, such as the seabed, a reef, or among seaweed, until it hatches. The design of the casing helps the egg to stay in place.

3. Some female sharks carry the eggs inside them to stop predators from eating the eggs. When ready, the eggs hatch inside the mother and then she gives birth to live pups. In some species, the pups will eat any unfertilized eggs while they are still inside their mother and sand tiger shark pups have been known to even eat each other before birth!

Penguin

There are at least seventeen species of penguin and most are found in the southern hemisphere, except for the Galápagos penguin, which resides on the tropical Galápagos Islands off the coast of South America.

Penguins can't fly and they aren't very stable on their feet, but they can certainly swim! Penguins are well equipped for swimming, with torpedo-shaped bodies, webbed feet and powerful wings that they use to glide through the water.

Penguins spend at least half their lives at sea. They hunt in the water and feed on prey such as krill (small, shrimp-like creatures), fish and squid. Most penguins can only hold their breath underwater for a few minutes, but the largest penguin – the emperor – can stay underwater for well over 20 minutes, diving to depths of over 550 metres (1,800 ft)!

The penguin's distinctive black-and-white appearance helps it to hide while it is in the water. However, the leopard seal (or sea leopard) will not be easily tricked. It lurks under the water before lunging at the bobbing penguins, snatching at them with its powerful jaws. This fierce predator may also wait near an ice shelf to snap at the penguins as they dive into the water.

Oceanic giants

The ocean is home to much larger creatures than those found on land. This is because sea animals don't have to support their own weight – the ocean water does that for them.

The largest animal in the world is the blue whale. In fact, it is the largest animal to have ever lived, with females of the species measuring up to 30 metres (98 ft) in length and weighing up to 180,000 kilograms (177 UK tons). Its tongue alone weighs as much as an elephant!

These enormous mammals feed almost exclusively on tiny krill, which they filter through a set of brush-like sieves in their mouths, known as "baleen plates". The whales suck in huge volumes of seawater in order to sieve out the food using the plates. This method means they can gulp large mouthfuls of food, instead of having to waste energy hunting a single meal. The blue whale can eat up to 40 million krill a day!

Most blue whales migrate to cold waters to find food and to warmer waters to breed and give birth. During their four-month migration, they eat very little, surviving mostly on the stores of food found in their fat, or "blubber".

Sensational sea slugs

Nudibranchs, or "sea slugs", are found in both warm and cold waters all around the world and at all depths. Their size ranges from just a few millimetres long to over 60 centimetres (24 in.). The largest species of nudibranch recorded is known as the "Spanish dancer".

About 3,000 different species of nudibranchs have currently been recorded, although it is believed that more are yet to be discovered. The chance of seeing a nudibranch in the ocean is fairly high, although they are masters of disguise. They use their famous and extraordinary coloured and patterned bodies – from stripes to polka dots – to blend in with their surroundings.

These carnivores can spend a lot of time feasting on brightly coloured sea sponges or anemones. The colour pigments from the nudibranch's food go into its skin so that it matches its prey and stays well hidden while feeding. Some species can also absorb the stinging cells (nematocysts) from their prey and use them later on against predators – you are what you eat if you're a nudibranch!

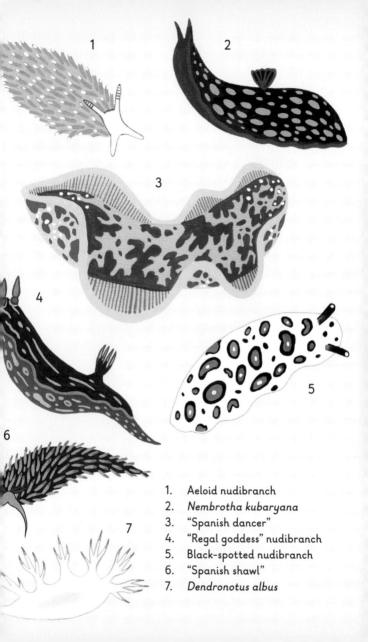

1. Aeloid nudibranch
2. *Nembrotha kubaryana*
3. "Spanish dancer"
4. "Regal goddess" nudibranch
5. Black-spotted nudibranch
6. "Spanish shawl"
7. *Dendronotus albus*

Bioluminescence

There is a particularly deep and dark part of the sea known as the "midnight zone". It is an environment with no sunlight, near-to-freezing temperatures, little oxygen and extremely high pressure. Any wildlife living here has to be very well adapted in order to survive.

Some of the deep-sea creatures have developed some form of bioluminescence – a chemical reaction in their bodies that creates light. Here are a few examples:

Some deep-sea jellyfish, like the Halitrephes maasi, dazzle like underwater fireworks as their bodies and tentacles light up. They usually travel without any light, so it is most likely used for defence.

When frightened, the vampire squid fires a gooey cloud of bioluminescent mucus to dazzle attackers, giving it the chance to escape.

Brittle stars use light to scare away predators or to hint that they might be toxic. They even use it to attract their predator's predator, a technique known as the "burglar-alarm effect"!

The female deep-sea anglerfish, or "sea devil", has a built-in fishing rod on her head, which she uses to lure prey close to her before snapping them up in her powerful jaws.

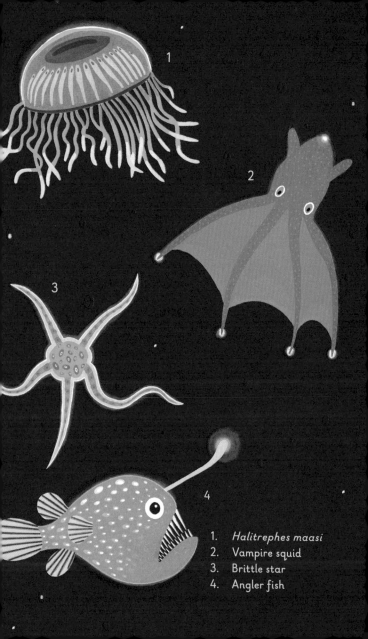

1. *Halitrephes maasi*
2. Vampire squid
3. Brittle star
4. Angler fish

A Ladybird Book

collectable books for curious kids

What to Look For in Spring

9780241416181

What to Look For in Summer

9780241416204

What to Look For in Autumn

9780241416167

What to Look For in Winter

9780241416228

SERIES 205

Animal Habitats

9780241416860

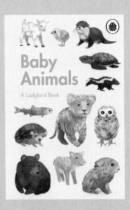

Baby Animals

9780241416907

Insects and Minibeasts

9780241417034

Trees

9780241417218

SERIES 208